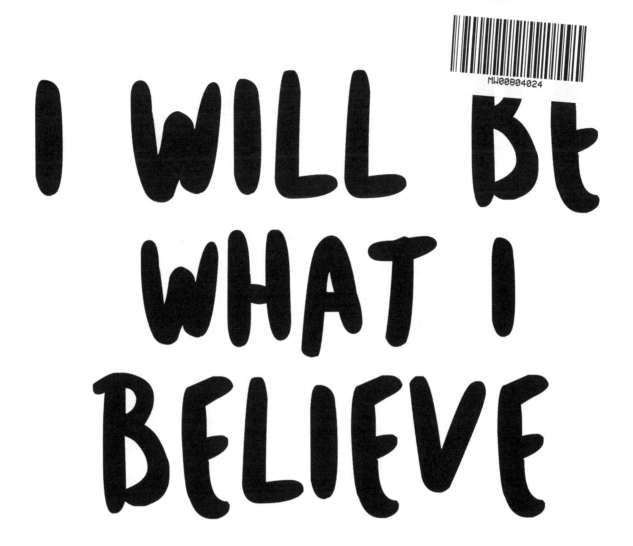

I WILL BE WHAT I BELIEVE

Blake Gillette

CFI, AN IMPRINT OF CEDAR FORT, INC.
SPRINGVILLE, UTAH

To my wife, Kaicie, and to my children,
Kennadee, Caden, and Maeser, for inspiring me to do it.

To my mother, Luann, for forcing me to play the piano—
it was worth the trial and tribulation.

To my sisters, Paula, Julie, and Fawna, for immersing me into music at an early age and
dragging me around town to all of their choir and music programs.

To Merrilee Webb for teaching me how to listen to, understand, and play music.

And to the Rochester Fourth and Mapleton Fourth Ward Primaries for actually liking
my songs and giving me the courage to keep writing and arranging new ones.

ISBN 13: 978-1-4621-2055-0 (Book)
ISBN 13: 978-1-4621-2080-2 (Book & CD)

Published by CFI, an imprint of Cedar Fort, Inc., 2373 W. 700 S., Springville, UT 84663
Distributed by Cedar Fort, Inc., www.cedarfort.com

Cover design by Kinsey Beckett and Jeff Harvey
Cover design © 2017 by Cedar Fort, Inc.
Edited and typeset by Chelsea Holdaway

Printed in the United States of America

10 9 8 7 6 5 4 3 2

Printed on acid-free paper

CONTENTS

I WILL BE WHAT I BELIEVE

Words and Music by
BLAKE GILLETTE
We'll Bring the World His Truth
JANICE KAPP PERRY

MY HEAVENLY FATHER LOVES ME / I FEEL MY SAVIOR'S LOVE

My Heavenly Father Loves Me
Words and Music by CLARA W. McMASTER
© by Intellectual Reserve, Inc.
I Feel My Savior's Love
Words by RALPH RODGERS JR.
Words and Music by K. NEWELL DAYLEY

Arranged by BLAKE GILLETTE

♩ = 78

glad that I live in this beau-ti-ful world Heav'n-ly Fa-ther___ cre-at-ed___ for me. I

feel my Sav-ior's love In all the world a-round me. His Spi-rit warms my

soul Through ev-'ry-thing I see. He knows I will fol-low him,

I KNOW THAT YOU LOVE ME

Words and Music by
BLAKE GILLETTE

BEHOLD YOUR LITTLE ONES

Words and Music by
BLAKE GILLETTE

Reverently

great was our faith._____ En - cir-cled by fire, an - gels com - ing down, A

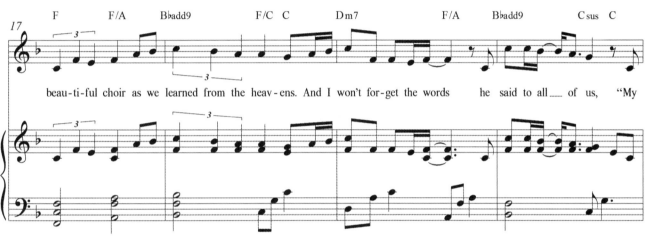

beau-ti-ful choir as we learned from the heav-ens. And I won't for-get the words he said to all__ of us, "My

joy is full. Be - hold_____ your lit-tle ones."____

I'LL KNOW FOR MYSELF

Words and Music by
BLAKE GILLETTE

Joseph Smith's First Prayer
Words by GEORGE MANWARING
Music by SYLVANUS BILLINGS POND

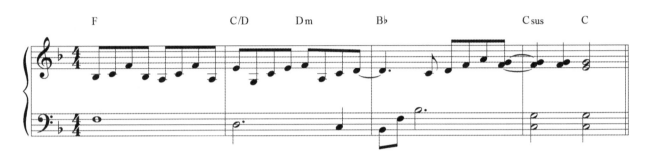

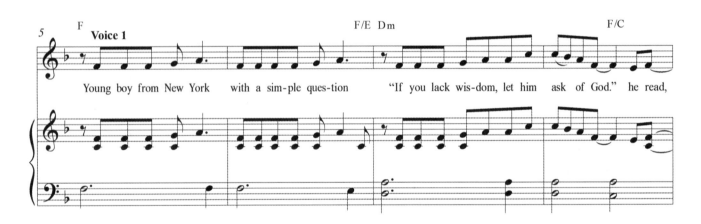

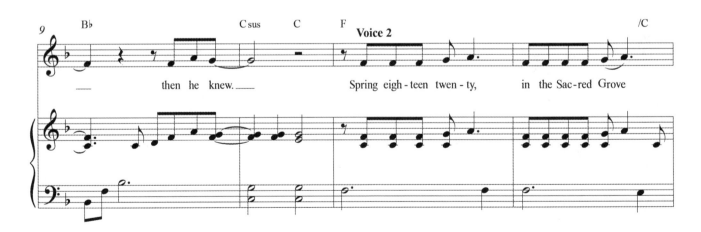

humble prayer was answered, And he listened to the Lord. While appeared two Heav'nly

beings, God the Father and the Son. Oh, what rapture filled his

bosom, For he saw the living God.

Mother's Day Mash-Up

Teach Me to Walk in the Light
Words and Music by CLARA W. McMASTER
© by Intellectual Reserve, Inc.
Love Is Spoken Here
Words and Music by JANICE KAPP PERRY

Arranged by
BLAKE GILLETTE

I see my moth - er kneel - ing with our

fam - i - ly each day. I hear the words she whis - pers as she bows her head to

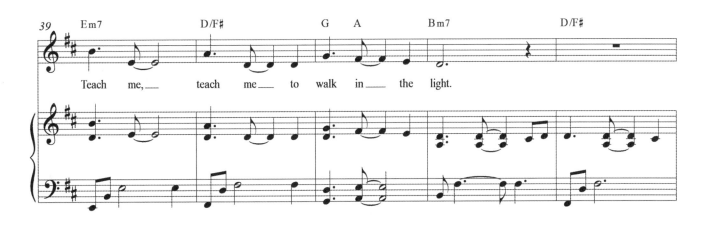

Teach me, __ teach me __ to walk in __ the light.

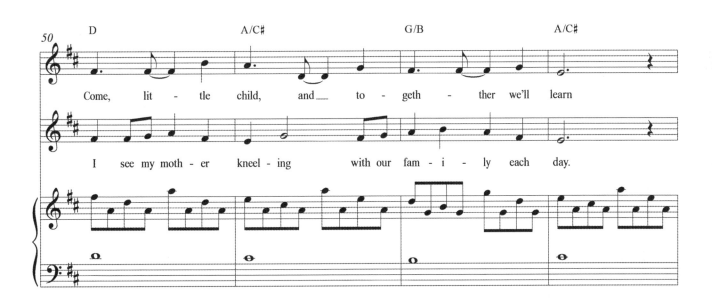

Come, lit - tle child, and __ to - geth - ther we'll learn

I see my moth - er kneel - ing with our fam - i - ly each day.

I see my moth - er kneel - ing.

Mine is a home.

One Eternal Round

Arranged by BLAKE GILLETTE

I Love to See the Temple
Music by JANICE KAPP PERRY
If You Could Hie to Kolob
Music: English Melody

* Other than this, you are on your own!

One eternal round.

WHEN HE COMES AGAIN / JOY TO THE WORLD

Arranged by
BLAKE GILLETTE

When He Comes Again
Words and Music by MIRLA GREENWOOD THAYNE
Joy to the World
Text by ISAAC WATTS
Music by GEORGE F. HANDEL

♩ = 94

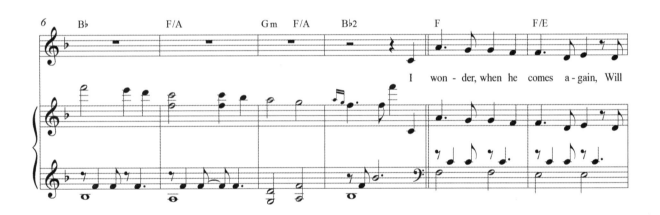

I won-der, when he comes a-gain, Will

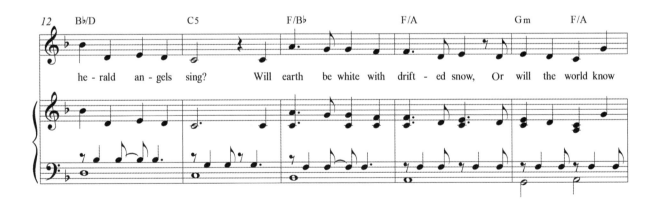

he-rald an-gels sing? Will earth be white with drift - ed snow, Or will the world know

when that bless-ed day is here, He'll love me and he'll say, "You've served me well, my lit - tle child;

Come un - to my arms to stay." Joy to the world, joy to the

world, the Lord is come; let earth re - ceive her King!

I LIVED IN HEAVEN

Arranged by
BLAKE GILLETTE

Words and Music by
JANEEN JACOBS BRADY

1. I lived in heav-en a long time a-go, it is true;
2. Fa-ther said he need-ed some-one who had e-nough love
3. Je-sus was cho-sen, and as the Mes-si-ah he came,

Lived there and loved there with peo-ple I know. So did you.
To give his life so we all could re-turn there a-bove.
Con-quer-ing e-vil and death through his glo-ri-ous name,

WE WELCOME YOU TODAY!

Words and Music by
BLAKE GILLETTE

I HOPE THEY CALL ME ON A MISSION / WE'LL BRING THE WORLD HIS TRUTH

Arranged by
BLAKE GILLETTE

I Hope They Call Me On a Mission
Words and Music by NEWEL KAY BROWN
© Intellectual Reserve, Inc.
We'll Bring the World His Truth
Words and Music by JANICE KAPP PERRY

bring the world his truth.

bring the world his truth.

For music tips and performance suggestions,
visit www.blakegillettemusic.com.